Original title:
On the Edge of the Ocean

Copyright © 2025 Creative Arts Management OÜ
All rights reserved.

Author: Fiona Harrington
ISBN HARDBACK: 978-1-80581-508-2
ISBN PAPERBACK: 978-1-80581-035-3
ISBN EBOOK: 978-1-80581-508-2

The Heartbeat of the Deep

Waves giggle as they dash,
While crabs hold a crabby bash.
The fish wear tiny hats,
Swapping tales of acrobatic spats.

Seagulls swoop with honks and flaps,
Dancing 'round like silly chaps.
With fins a-flip and tails a-flare,
They pull off moves beyond compare.

Curved Lines of the Wandering Surf

The tide tickles with a gentle tease,
Shells sing songs that float on breeze.
A turtle plays hide and seek,
In seaweed, it finds its sneak peek.

An octopus twirls in a whirl,
While starfish jiggle, begin to twirl.
Their laughter bubbles with salty cheer,
Creating waves of giggles near.

Where the Sun Meets the Water

Flamingos stroll in stylish shoes,
Waving as they sip their brews.
The sun dips low on the horizon line,
While fishes sigh, 'This is divine!'

Beach balls bounce with frothy cheers,
Chasing shadows, facing fears.
With laughter echoing through the sands,
Splashes drum from joyful hands.

Sketches of Seaglass and Dolphin Dreams

Dolphins leap with sporty grace,
Performing flips in a splashy race.
With seaglass glinting in the sun,
The beach is where the fun's begun.

Sandcastles melt like dreams at night,
As crabs paint patterns in delight.
With each wave, a new tale to blend,
In the whims of the ocean's end.

Dancing Shadows in Dusk's Embrace

Twilight giggles, shadows play,
Seagulls swoop, then fly away.
Laughter echoes, as waves roll,
Flip-flops dance, with spirits whole.

Bubbles pop like joyful dreams,
Sandcastles wobble at their seams.
Carefree folks with ice cream scoops,
Join the waltz with ocean loops.

Driftwood Dreams and Salty Songs

Driftwood battles—who will win?
A crab with swagger, cheeky grin.
Seashell trumpets call the crew,
Join the chorus, sing anew.

Tomatoes float on frothy waves,
As we surf on pickled caves.
A fish in shades of purple hue,
Claims the title: 'Best Dancer Too!'

Echoes of the Distant Tide

Waves whisper jokes we can't quite catch,
A dolphin jokes, with quite a snatch.
Shells giggle as the tide retreats,
While sand crabs shake their tiny feet.

Wind chimes laugh in the salty breeze,
The seaweed winks at clumsy knees.
Plankton paint the ocean floor,
Telling tales of long-lost lore.

Reflections in the Seafoam Light

Mirrors shimmer, reflections tease,
Bubbles burst, it's hard to please!
Sandy toes and knotted hair,
We giggle at the salty air.

A fish dons shades, like it's a pro,
While starfish strike a beachy show.
Laughter dances with the foam,
As we chase the sunset home.

Riding the Wind's Whisper

The seagulls squawk and dive for fries,
While beachgoers dance in sunscreen guise.
A crab in shades scuttles with flair,
Chasing a sandwich—what a real scare!

The sun's a ball of melting cheese,
While kids surf on waves with gleeful ease.
Sandcastles topple, they yell with glee,
"That's not our fort, it's a sand tsunami!"

Glistening Shores and Ghostly Whispers

The lighthouse winks with a blinking light,
While ghost crabs giggle and scuttle out of sight.
A fishing pole trips, a man takes a splash,
As a wave roars by with a mischievous crash.

A mermaid lounges, called in by the tide,
With seashell earrings and fish as her guide.
She's giving advice on how to catch waves,
But the fish just laugh, no help could they save!

Memory Lane by the Ocean's Side

Tanned tourists wobble on rented boards,
While parents yell, "Don't paddle towards the hoards!"
A beach ball soars, hits a man in the face,
He's now part of the surf, what a comical case!

The ice cream truck lags, stuck in the sand,
While kids build a tunnel, it's not quite planned.
"Hey, watch out!" screams a girl, what's the point?
Down goes an adult—now he's just a joint!

Radiance of the Twilight Foam

The sun dips low, like a goldfish in flight,
With flamingos posing, what a silly sight!
A starfish grins, it's well aware,
Of beachgoers racing without a care.

As twilight nudges the foam to a glow,
The jellyfish leashes float to and fro.
A crab's throwing parties—he's quite the host,
With sand-salsa dancing, who could complain most?

A Sailor's Soliloquy

I set my course with a bumpy grin,
The wind is wild, let the antics begin!
A hat flies off, I chase it with glee,
Turns out that was my lunch, oh dear me!

The fish are laughing, as I cartwheel around,
With a splash and a crash, I'm lost and I'm found.
Ropes tie me up, like a sailor in plight,
But who needs control when you've got such a sight?

Rugged Cliffs and Quiet Currents

Waves crash and giggle, they think it's a game,
As I slip on a rock, oh what a shame.
Seagulls cackle, they chant at my fall,
I'd call for help, but I'm too proud to crawl.

With seaweed in hand, I do my best dance,
The fish roll their eyes, I don't stand a chance.
Nature's my stage, I take center floor,
But all I can muster is a face full of shore!

Secrets of the Deep Blue

Bubbles arise, like secrets that laugh,
A crab in a tux knows it's a silly gaffe.
Underwater whispers, a jellyfish grins,
"Come join our party, let the fun begin!"

I tried to dive deep, but what did I find?
A shoal of fish teasing, "You're losing your mind!"
They twirl in circles, I float in dismay,
Who knew ocean life could be so cliché?

The Restless Shoreline's Song

The tide pulls my shoes, oh what a grand heist,
As I chase after shoes, it's quite a wild feast.
Sand tickles my toes, giggles in the breeze,
With a bucket of crabs plotting my unease.

Waves crashing in jest, I'm caught in their play,
They sneak up on me, trying to steal the day.
A sandcastle fortress, but the tide has its say,
"Not today, my friend, I'm here for your stay!"

The Solace of Salted Air

The gulls squawk loud, a raucous cheer,
As I chase crabs, they scuttle near.
With sandy toes and hair like hay,
I swear I'll catch one - but they betray.

The sun beats down, my ice cream melts,
A sticky mess, can't blame the pelts.
I take a lick, it drips on my knee,
Seagulls laugh, oh sweet irony!

Reflections in the Ocean's Gaze

I saw myself in water blue,
A goofy grin, a wild hairdo.
The waves come in, they splash and tease,
My pants are soaked, Oh, what a breeze!

A fish swims by, it gives a wink,
I hold my breath, then start to sink.
Pop up and wipe the salty spray,
Who needs a mirror? I'm here to play!

Dancing Shadows on Soft Sands

The shadows stretch, they twirl and spin,
As I attempt to move, to grin.
A flip-flop flies, hits a beach ball,
And I perform my greatest fall!

A dog runs by, steals my snack,
Chasing after, I lose my track.
The sand is hot, my feet do scream,
But the laughter's worth it, it seems.

Dreams of Sailboats and Sunset Glows

The boats bob gently, sails like hats,
I dream of voyages, adventures, and chats.
But here comes a wave, strong and bold,
I tip over, my dreams on hold!

I swim back to shore, with grace I'm not,
Where tiny fish nibble at my spot.
"Well, at least," I say, "it's just for fun!"
As they nibble on toes, I feel like a pun!

Driftwood Tales Beneath the Moon

A log once claimed to be a boat,
Quite confident, it tried to float.
It laughed at waves with such a glee,
Yet stayed right there, poor splintered tree.

The crabs held court, all dressed in shells,
Telling tall tales with swishy swells.
They shared their dreams of gliding free,
But had no plans beyond a spree.

Embracing the Boundless Abyss

A jellyfish with a fancy hat,
Twirled and danced, so cool and flat.
It startled fish with its grand show,
While they rolled eyes, not impressed though.

A clam dreamed big of being a star,
But never left its cozy jar.
It wished to sing, but feared the tide,
Instead it hummed and just sighed wide.

Windswept Hearts and Mysterious Depths

Seagulls compete in a diving race,
Flapping wildly, what a wild chase!
One got stuck in a child's chip bag,
Claiming it's now a stylish rag.

The dolphins laughed at the fishy chase,
Launching high, with such finesse and grace.
Yet one got tangled in a seaweed thread,
And wore it proudly, a crown on its head.

A Canvas of Seagulls and Salt

Seagulls painted with splashes of spice,
Drew funny faces, oh, what a slice!
They posed by the waves with a cheeky grin,
Mocking the surfers trying to win.

The tide brought stories like drifting sand,
Tales of sea monsters, and ghostly bands.
Just a crab chuckled, with a wink and a wave,
"Honestly, my friends, let's just misbehave!"

Songs Carried by the Wind

Seagulls sing a comical tune,
As crabs dance beneath the bright moon.
A fish slipped on a slippery scale,
Told the dolphin, 'Do not tell a tale!'

The wind whispers secrets so bold,
Of mermaids with hair made of gold.
They giggle as they splash and play,
Stealing shells from the beach each day.

A crab with a hat struts on the sand,
Claiming the title of the wisest in the land.
With laughter echoing across the bay,
Try catching fish? They're just here to play!

So let your laughter be free and wild,
As the ocean waves tease like a child.
With each wave a giggle, a splash, a grin,
The songs of the sea make us all dive in!

The Dance of Fishermen's Nets

Fishermen twirl their nets with flair,
Throwing lines without a single care.
One tangled up, the other fell flat,
The fish are laughing, how about that?

Their boats wobble, a comedic sight,
As they chase fish that playfully bite.
With lines all crossed, and hooks entwined,
They're champions of the bumbling kind!

The seaweed wraps around their feet,
They tumble and keep missing their seat.
But with each cast, their spirits stay high,
For even mishaps bring joy to the sky!

So let the nets fly like caps in the air,
In a laughable dance, without a care.
The ocean's humor, a swell of delight,
Turn each fishing trip into a merry plight!

Elysium Beneath the Waves

Deep below where the seaweed sways,
Lies a kingdom of fish in funny displays.
With bubbles and giggles, they swim with glee,
Creating stories for all to see.

A octopus juggles, six balls at once,
While a starfish waits, looking like a dunce.
They throw a party for every fish near,
Inviting a shark, who just grinned from ear to ear.

The sea cucumbers dance with great flair,
While the clownfish blush, too shy to compare.
They spin in circles, a bubble parade,
This wacky world where laughter won't fade.

So plunge into laughter beneath the blue,
With creatures performing just for you.
Elysium awaits where fun never stops,
In this watery realm, joy bubbles and hops!

The Soft Murmurs of a Distant Tide

Whispers of the sea drift like a breeze,
Tickling the shells, making them sneeze.
A crab wearing glasses peers at the shore,
"Is that a potato? I'm not sure anymore!"

Waves crash and giggle, a foamy delight,
As the shoreline wears a frothy white sight.
A fish in a tux, trying hard to look grand,
Tipped his top hat, but fell in the sand.

Each splash a joke, each ripple a grin,
As dolphins perform, without any din.
They flip and they flounder, winning applause,
A comedy show where laughter has no pause.

So listen closely to each rolling wave,
Their whispers of fun, the joy that we crave.
With every murmur, let giggles resound,
In the softest rhythm where humor is found!

The Last Song of the Setting Sun

The sun hums low with a wink,
As seagulls dance and blink,
Sirens sing with a playful strum,
While crabs throw sand in a joyful drum.

Wave after wave begins to tease,
Chasing each other with a splash and wheeze,
A starfish claims the best front row seat,
While dolphins giggle and shuffle their feet.

Beneath the giggle of the tide,
Shells gossip as the lovers collide,
The horizon blushes in crimson delight,
While fish plot their escape from the night.

So let the evening's laughter rise,
In this sandy spot beneath the skies,
Where even the moon leans in to hear,
The last song sung to the shoreline near.

Footprints in the Glistening Sand

Tiny toes leave trails so bold,
In sunshine that never grows old,
A sandcastle stands, though half a mess,
With a moat that's formed from a kid's distress.

Dogs in the water, chasing their tails,
While kids sell seashells with exaggerated tales,
Each footstep whispers secrets and plays,
Of ice cream dreams and ocean frays.

The sandy shores are a canvas bright,
Footprints left in a messy delight,
With giggles echoing through the warm air,
As the sun grins, tossing its golden hair.

So let's be silly, let's roll around,
With laughter bouncing off the ground,
These footprints we leave will surely withstand,
The playful tricks of our glistening land.

Currents of a Forgotten Memory

A tide pool dances, a swirling mess,
With crabs that seem to play chess,
Old barnacles wear glasses, so wise,
While octopuses charm with their sly guise.

The whispers of jellyfish float by,
As dolphins try to sing to the sky,
A beat-up buoy dreams of days gone past,
As whispers turn to giggles at last.

Sand dollars converse about grand designs,
While sea cucumbers share silly lines,
Each wave recalls a story untold,
Of barnacle romances and treasures of old.

Let's raise a toast to the fishy crew,
Who share our secrets, fickle and true,
Waves of memories twirl and glide,
In the watery depths where we all reside.

A Canvas of Blue and Gold

Strokes of blue splash through the air,
While seagulls laugh without a care,
A painter's palette spills on the shore,
With colors bright we can't ignore.

Golden rays tickle the surface tight,
As surfers tumble with glee and slight,
Each curl of foam is a playful friend,
The canvas expands, it never ends.

Kites soar high, a funny parade,
While laughter echoes through the cascade,
The horizon blinks, paints stories bold,
In this gallery where joy unfolds.

So let's create with every single wave,
A masterpiece in every brave,
With splashes of fun and joy to behold,
This canvas of blue and gold.

Quicksands of Time and Memory

Footprints vanish, they play hide and seek,
As tides sweep in, they go sneak peek.
With each wave's laugh, I try to keep track,
But my shoes keep sinking, oh, what a knack!

Shells whisper secrets from days gone by,
A clam full of jokes, oh my, oh my!
The seaweed dances, a wiggly prank,
While seagulls cackle, their wings in a crank.

Floating in memories, I paddle and trot,
Castles of sand that I built on the spot.
But the tide comes rushing, a thief in the night,
And all that's left is a soggy delight!

So here I stand, with a smile and a shrug,
Embracing the chaos, feeling the tug.
For time is a wave, both silly and grand,
And laughter's the treasure buried in sand.

Navigating the Labyrinth of the Seaside

Maps made of candy, the shoreline so sweet,
I wander the twists with my flip-flop feet.
A crab with a compass shows me the way,
But points to a picnic where someone can play.

Pails full of jellybeans instead of sand,
Seagulls on stilts in a marching band.
I get lost in laughter, not worried at all,
When a dolphin shouts, 'Hey, come join the ball!'

The maze made of kelp has a slippery slide,
Each corner I turn, there's a splash and a glide.
Shells with a wink, they giggle and tease,
As I chase after whispers carried by breeze.

So here's to getting tangled in mirth,
Finding joy in the mess, that's what it's worth!
With a chuckle and cheer, I dance with delight,
In this seaside puzzle, I'm lost, but it's right!

Moonlit Secrets of the Waters Edge

Under the glow of a prankster moon,
The sea tells tales in a giggling tune.
Stars wink and wiggle, a humorous sight,
As fish don hats, preparing for night!

Crabs throw a party on soft sandy floors,
With sandcastles standing, guarding the shores.
They dance with the waves, a slippery ball,
And invite all the stars to a shimmering call.

The tide rolls in with a belly full of bliss,
Each splash a secret, each wave a kiss.
I join in the chorus, a giggle or two,
As secrets of water ripple into view.

So let's lift our voices to the playful tide,
Where laughter and waves swirl side by side.
With moonlit whispers, let joy take flight,
As the ocean chuckles beneath starlit night.

Whispers of the Tidal Breeze

The gulls take bets on my sandwich,
They circle like thieves in the sun.
I wave my arms, they cackle back,
It's hard to stay mad when you're having fun.

Seagulls squabble for popcorn snacks,
While crabs dance like kings on the sand.
I laugh as they prance, claws waving,
Who knew crustaceans had such a band?

The waves chase shadows, then retreat,
I trip on a shell and fall like a clown.
The fish wink at me from beneath,
Giggling as I flail my way down.

With each splash, laughter breaks free,
The ocean's laughter fills the air.
I join in the chorus of joyful noise,
Who knew sun and sea could be so rare?

Beyond the Horizon's Veil

A dolphin pops up with a grin,
As if to say, 'Come play, my friend!'
I toss him my frisbee — oh no! —
He better not bring that to a swim meet!

The sun winks down with a mischievous gleam,
While sandcastles crumble at every wave.
I watch my moat turn into a stream,
The tide has no respect for the brave!

A beach ball drifts out to sea,
I shake my fist, it laughs with glee.
The ocean knows how to prank, it seems,
But I suppose it's just living its dreams.

As flip-flops dance in the breeze,
I'm tripped by a wave that's clumsy and bold.
With every tumble, my laughter just grows,
The horizon's absent, but joy's never old.

Where Waves Meet the Sky

The tide pulls back like a shy child,
Only to leap forward with full delight.
I watch my toes get swallowed whole,
The ocean's tickles make quite a sight!

A jellyfish floats, oh what a show,
It waves its tentacles as if saying, 'Hi!'
I dive to escape its gentle hug,
But end up with a splash and a pie in the sky.

Shells whisper secrets, shhh, listen close,
They gossip about crabs and their newest dance.
I join the party, shells underfoot,
The beach is alive with mischief and chance!

With each new wave, laughter ensues,
Who knew the ocean could tease so well?
I leave my worries on the wet sand,
And dive into stories that splashes tell.

The Silent Shoreline's Secret

On this quiet stretch where the surf hums,
Sandcastles sit like neglected kings.
A starfish waves with all of its arms,
It's clearly playing, not worrying of things.

The tide pulls toys into its watery vault,
I chase after hope with a squeaky toy.
The gulls see the fun and join the assault,
I'm now a live target for their envoy.

There's a beach ball lost in the distance,
With flavors of sunscreen and errant sun.
It rolls on the surface, just out of reach,
Reminding me how a good chase is fun!

As the sun sets low, painting the sky,
I giggle at memories of seafoam and cheer.
With laughter echoing all around,
The secrets of the shore always end in beer!

Colors of the Dusk: An Oceanic Symphony

Seagulls squawk like honking cars,
While crabs dance under the stars.
A fish wears a hat, quite absurd,
Swims by with nary a word.

Waves giggle, tickle the supine sand,
Shells gossip about their sunbaked land.
A starfish paints its toes in hues,
While dolphins play hopscotch with snooze.

The tide holds a party at twilight's door,
Mermaids sing, 'Who ordered more?'
Floating snacks, jellyfish weightless,
The ocean's a buffet, quite tasteless!

Crabs in tuxedos waltz to the beat,
While an octopus serves up a treat.
With laughter echoing under the sun,
Each splash a cheer, oh what fun!

The Flight of Dreams Over Water's Whisper

A pelican dreams with a fishy grin,
Thinking of ways to sneakily win.
Seagulls throw shade, oh what a scene,
While they barter for chips, oh the cuisine!

Waves weave tales of calamitous trips,
As a walrus does cannonballs, flips.
Bottles bob in a nautical dance,
The ocean's not shy, just taking a chance.

Sunburnt folk sip their coconut cups,
While jellyfish float like fluffy pups.
The breeze steals hats and a wave gives chase,
All in good fun, at a frenzied pace.

And as the sun bids goodnight,
Fish-in-flip-flops take flight.
With laughter ringing, the night is bright,
In dreams, they'll dance til the morning light!

Whispers of the Tidal Breeze

The tides have secrets they love to share,
Like how crabs play tag without a care.
Seashells gossip about their bling,
While a clownfish practices its swing.

Old fishermen weave stories bold,
Of mermaids that made them feel old.
A dolphin with sunglasses rides the swell,
Hilarious tales, can you tell?

The sun dips down with a wink and grin,
While fish explore their wildest spin.
With every wave, laughter's released,
As silly sea creatures join the feast.

So let the breeze take you for a ride,
Amongst the waves where giggles abide.
To this watery world, we all belong,
In this silly symphony, life's a song!

Sandcastles and Forgotten Dreams

Once I built a castle high,
With a moat that made me sigh.
But waves came in to take a bite,
Now I'm left with just sand in sight.

I put a flag atop my throne,
But seagulls found it all alone.
They squawk and laugh as tides roll in,
While I just muse where I begin.

Children play and laugh out loud,
While I blend in like a cloud.
With sunscreen smeared upon my nose,
I dig for treasures, no one knows.

Each wave that rushes to the shore,
Makes me wish for just one more.
But sand's a fickle friend you see,
It laughs and says, "Come play with me!"

Twilight Reflections on Rippled Waters

In the twilight, shadows grow,
The crabs put on quite a show.
They dance beneath the fading light,
While I stumble, what a sight!

The sun dips low, a tomato red,
I accidentally step on Fred.
The crab looks mad, then scuttles fast,
I promise him I'll change at last.

Ripples laugh as I lose my flip,
To a wave that does a little dip.
I chase it down with floppy feet,
And slip again—it's a wet retreat!

The moon comes up, it's quite a tease,
Makes the water glimmer with ease.
But while I dream of fish and fun,
The tide just shows, "You're not the one!"

Celestial Dance of Stars and Sea

Stars twinkle down like popcorn bright,
While I stumble through the night.
The waves keep laughing, what a sight,
As I try to dance—oh, what a plight!

A starfish winks, says, "Join the fun!"
But I trip over my own pun.
The ocean whispers silly jokes,
While I just grin, surrounded by folks.

Jellyfish float with a graceful flair,
I ponder if they even care.
A splash of water and I'm awake,
The ocean's laugh, my silly mistake!

In this cosmic dance of sheer delight,
I ponder deep and hold on tight.
The stars above and sea below,
They giggle well, as tides will flow.

A Journey Through Mist and Foam

Fog rolls in, like breakfast steam,
Misty mornings, a dreamer's theme.
I wander forth, feeling quite bold,
Only to find I've lost my hold!

The foam tickles my toes, so sly,
"This isn't the way!" I cry and sigh.
But surfboards zoom past like a ghost,
Laughing at me, I'm quite the host!

As mist surrounds, I start to roam,
Imagine waves as my own home.
A pelican swoops down with flair,
I'm now the target of its glare!

Through foam and mist, I seek the path,
While the ocean bubbles, and makes me laugh.
Oh, what a journey, filled with charms,
Who knew that waves could also disarm?

Where Land Meets Liquid Infinity

Waves giggle on the shore,
As seagulls dance and soar.
Flip-flops fly with each splash,
And picnic ants make a dash.

Sandy shoes, a comical sight,
As children squeal with delight.
Buckets tip over, ice cream spills,
While crabs march like they're paying bills.

A beach ball bounces high and low,
As sunbathers chase it to and fro.
With sunscreen on just like a clown,
They learn quickly not to frown.

Castles built with pride and care,
Only to be claimed by air.
Salty laughs and endless play,
Who knew the sea could be so gay?

The Call of the Foamy Frontier

A surfboard whispers to the shore,
And waves debate who'll score.
Will it be the kid with no fear?
Or the dog who's a shipwrecked seer?

Flip-flops stuck, the lifeguard grins,
As tanned tourists dive on whims.
Mermaids giggle, a scale or two,
As crabs take selfies in the blue.

A rubber duck floats with a frown,
While jellyfish dress up like a clown.
The tide pulls back, a comical tease,
As sea cucumbers whisper "Please!"

Beach chairs in a kite-like fight,
As wind pays a surprise visit, quite.
Oh, the blunders of sun-filled days,
In this wavy, laughter-filled maze!

Beneath the Sunlit Veil

Sandy paths where jelly beans grow,
And starfish put on quite a show.
Beach umbrellas marching in lines,
As seagulls trade their cheesy pines.

A crab in sunglasses struts with flair,
While mermaids giggle without a care.
Kids chase foam with squeals and shouts,
And sandcastles develop clout.

Picnics settle with ants on a spree,
Biting into sandwiches as big as a tree.
Umbrellas flip with a gusty cheer,
While flotillas of ducks waddle near.

Naps are missed with too much glee,
As flip-flops dance to the sea's symphony.
Time flies fast on this sandy trail,
In a world where laughter cannot fail!

Echoes of Shells and Shadows

Shells clatter across the shore,
As beachgoers pretend to snore.
The sea swirls in mischievous tone,
With a seaweed hat like a throne.

Children laughing, buckets in hand,
Chasing the tide, forming a band.
Spots of sunblock, a ghostly white,
As seagulls plot their comical flight.

A wave crashes down with a shout,
While a fisherman's line goes about.
Twisted tales of catches grand,
While feisty crabs clutch at the sand.

At dusk, the shadows stretch and play,
As lanterns flicker to light the way.
The echoes of laughter sparkle in foam,
In a land that feels just like home!

Resting Above the Abyss

Seagulls squawk and dive around,
I'm perched on rocks, feeling quite proud.
The waves crash in, a rhythmic dance,
A fish jumps high, missing my pants.

A crab scuttles, pinching my toes,
While I wave at tourists in their rows.
Thoughts on the snacks I left behind,
Next to my towel, what a bind!

Sunscreen all over, what's this mess?
I'm a beach whale, I must confess.
The tide rolls in, I start to slide,
Cannonball splash, now I'm the tide!

Floating high as laughter rings,
In my dreams, I grow tiny wings.
The ocean laughs, 'Come join the fun,'
I'd race a dolphin—if I could run!

Gazing into Liquid Memories

Waves whisper secrets, quite absurd,
Shells tell tales, but they're so blurred.
I squint at fish with googly eyes,
Playing hide and seek, what a surprise!

The sun's a frying pan, so bright,
I'm sizzling up like morning light.
My ice cream cone, oh what a sight,
Melting fast in the heat—pure fright!

A sandcastle built with love and care,
Until a wave giggles, 'Not so fair!'
It topples down, my masterpiece gone,
But let's build more—come, carry on!

My straw hat flies, a gust so bold,
Chasing it down, a sight to behold.
Splashing through puddles, oh what glee,
Life's little comedy right by the sea!

Reflections on a Shimmering Tide

The sun sets down, a disco ball,
I practice my dance, but take a fall.
Splashing about, with laughter so bright,
Who knew the sea could put up a fight?

Flipping my towel like a cape in flight,
Pretending to be a superhero tonight.
But sand sticks on like it's super glue,
My cape is a mess, but I feel brand new!

Flip-flops flying, what a great chase,
I'd throw them back, but that's just disgrace.
A sea turtle laughs with a wink so sly,
'You're out in the sea, just let it fly!'

With every wave, I jump and cheer,
The ocean's my stage, the end is near.
But oh, the joy of the splish and splash,
In this silly dance, I'm making a splash!

Sand Between My Toes and Stars Above

Under the stars, I lie with glee,
Counting grains, one—there goes my knee!
The moon lights up my sandy domain,
With each wave crashing, it calls my name.

A hermit crab, with tiny bling,
Sneaks past my flip-flops like a king.
'Excuse me, buddy, you're in my zone,'
I must say, I'm not a fan of crabs alone!

The air is salty, my hair's a mess,
I'd trade it all for a little less stress.
But here on the shore, all joys combine,
In sand castles and flip-flops, I'll always shine.

And if the stars decide to fall,
We'll catch them all, no need to stall.
With laughter echoing far and wide,
We'll dance together, just let it slide!

Boundless Depths and Sandy Realms

Seagulls squawk and play, oh what a sight,
Chasing waves like children, pure delight.
Fish wear sunglasses, sipping on brine,
While crabs in cool shades dance out of line.

Waves crash like laughter, splashes abound,
Flip-flops flying off, lost in the sound.
Jellyfish float by, wearing hats too wide,
As the ocean giggles, it can't even hide.

The Breath of the Infinite Waters

The tide whispers secrets with salty breath,
Inviting all sunbathers to join the quest.
Starfish do the cha-cha on the sunlit sand,
While old crabs gossip, forming a band.

Octopuses juggle, putting on a show,
They flip their tentacles, stealing the glow.
Seashells are troopers, marching in line,
Saying, 'Hey, little buddy, aren't we divine?'

Shoreline Reveries Under Starlit Skies

Under the stars, the creatures take flight,
Frogs croon sweet nothings, all through the night.
Sandcastles giggle, wearing mud pie crowns,
While the tide pulls back, revealing their frowns.

Moonbeams are dancing on the waves' twisty crest,
Fish in tuxedos claim they look best.
The ocean's a show-off with a shimmering grin,
As the beach party starts, let the fun begin!

Where the Sea Kisses the Land

Where land meets the laughter of playful dreams,
A pelican snores, or so it seems.
Driftwood declares it's found new fame,
While barnacles giggle, they love the acclaim.

Sand dunes are loungers, soaking in rays,
Competing with waves in their sun-soaked displays.
Seashells conspire, plotting a game,
Laughing and singing, 'It's all the same!'

Far Beyond the Coastal Mirage

Seagulls squawk, they steal my fries,
As I shout, they just apologize.
Shells collect, a treasure hunt,
But crabs just scuttled, not a single blunt.

Waves lapping, they tickle my toes,
I trip and tumble, oh how it goes!
With sandy hair and a crooked grin,
My beach day antics, where do I begin?

Sunburned nose, a lobster's hue,
Kids scream, the ice cream's all askew.
A sandcastle crumbles, the tide's a cheat,
Looks like this vacation is quite the feat!

But laughter bubbles with the salty breeze,
As I chase my hat up the swaying trees.
With buddies near and jokes to share,
This trip, my friends, has been quite rare!

Radiant Dawn on Pebbled Beach

Morning glow, the beach is mine,
But wait, what's this? A seagull's wine?
It swoops and dives, what a silly sight,
A squabble over crumbs, a feathery fight.

Pebbles roll, like marbles tossed,
In the race to find, oh what a cost!
A surfer's start, a wobbly pose,
He flips and flops, but nobody knows.

Salty snacks, a feast bizarre,
Chips and dips beneath the stars.
I spill my soda, watch it fizz,
And laugh as waves steal summer's quiz.

Friends all chuckle, on blankets we sprawl,
A sunburn parade, the best of all.
With giggles and glances, the fun won't end,
In this shining moment, we all transcend.

In the Shadow of a Distant Wave

A wave rolls in, then back again,
A strange little dance, let's try to pretend.
I splash and squeal, the water's cold,
Then trip on a floatie—oh, I am bold!

Kids build shrines, to all things grand,
While I just search for a reclined sand.
A beach ball bounces, I duck and weave,
Only to end up tangled in seaweed.

Sandwiches fly on the picnic table,
As gulls conspire, oh how they're able!
In the chaos, we shout and cheer,
It's the best of fun; we have no fear!

With sunburns and giggles, we dance in glee,
Collecting memories, as wild as a spree.
Each wave that crashes is a chance to play,
In our silly world, where laugh lines stay.

Requiem for the Wistful Tide

The tide rolls in, with secrets to share,
But she just tickles, with nary a care.
Surfers fall with a splash and a cheer,
Their laughter echoes, banishing fear.

A beach ball bounces, high in the air,
Missed by my buddy, but he does not care.
He runs after it, like a deer in flight,
Only to trip and disappear from sight.

Seashells scatter, a glittering mess,
I gather them all, yet find I'm no less.
With sand all over, like a badge of pride,
I declare a day that we'll never hide!

As sunset beckons with vibrant hues,
Our hearts are light, we share our views.
With whimsies cradled in the dusk's soft glow,
We'll laugh at the tales that the tide may bestow.

Salt and Serenity in Twilight's Embrace

A seagull stole my sandwich,
It flew away with glee,
I waved my arms like mad,
It seemed to laugh at me.

The sun begins to dip,
While children scream and play,
Their ice cream drips like magic,
And seagulls swoop in gray.

Sandcastles rise and tumble,
As tides play hide and seek,
With each wave, they whisper,
"Come join us for a peek!"

But days like this are fleeting,
Like bubbles in the breeze,
We chase them, oh so gladly,
With laughter, hearts at ease.

The Dance of the Gulls at Dusk

A flock of gulls in frenzy,
They twirl like dancers bold,
With flapping wings and squawking,
Their antics never old.

They dive for crumbs from picnics,
A circus in the skies,
While kids run, squealing loudly,
Watching with wide eyes.

The sunset paints the water,
In shades of orange groove,
The gulls chase after sunset,
In rhythm, they all move.

If only I could join them,
In flight upon the breeze,
But alas, my feet are planted,
At least I've got some cheese!

Temptation of the Untamed Waves

Those waves call out so loudly,
I swear they have a plan,
To pull me in their laughter,
And wash away the sand.

I ponder all the stories,
Of fish with tiny hats,
And mermaids sipping soda,
While called by silly chats.

A wave comes crashing closer,
And sprays my toes with foam,
I think I see a dolphin,
Shouting, "You're not alone!"

Each splash is pure temptation,
To frolic, jump, and play,
But I'll just stick to sunbathing,
And watch them swim away.

Secrets Buried Beneath the Drift

I found a shoe, a treasure,
Left by a pirate's ghost,
I checked inside for messages,
And laughed, it held a toast!

Beneath the rocks and seaweed,
Lie wonders great and small,
Including rubber duckies,
And notes from one and all.

With each wave's gentle lapping,
New secrets rise to shore,
Where flip-flops make good anchors,
And dreams are never poor.

So let the tide reveal them,
With giggles in the light,
For every oddball find here,
Is worth a laugh tonight!

The Horizon's Gentle Invitation

A seagull stole my sandwich, oh what a thief!
I waved my arms, feeling disbelief.
He squawked at me like I was a fool,
As I chased him down, looking like a tool.

The sun was bright, it made me squint,
I tried to look cool, but my hat had a hint.
It flew away like a bird in flight,
Now I'm hatless, oh what a sight!

Children laugh as they splash and play,
I trip on sand, with quite the display.
The bucket's tipping, the castle's caving,
I shout out loud, "I'm just misbehaving!"

The horizon beckons with a beckoning cheer,
I can't tell if it's the waves or my beer.
Still, I'll jump in, hair wild and free,
Life's too short; just drink sea foam tea!

Where Waves Kiss the Shore

Flip-flops flying, oh what a leap!
I thought I'd glide, instead I took a heap.
The tide rolled in, and so did my fate,
The sand stuck to me, my skin's second mate.

An ice cream cone melting in my hand,
I tried to lick it, but oh, it just planned.
It dripped down my chin, a sugary mess,
Yelled, "Cone please hold, don't you depress!"

Sunscreen applied like a buttered toast,
I'm shining bright, but I'm a ghost everyone can boast.
I slip and skid on the golden sands,
Like a clumsy dancer in slapstick bands.

The waves crash in with a foamy laugh,
I pretend to surf, oh what a gaffe!
But as I wipe out, I'm filled with glee,
Nothing is better than being sea foam free!

Footprints Lost to the Tides of Time

I wrote my name in the sand with pride,
Turned away for a snack, watched it subside.
The ocean's giggles are all too real,
As it washed away, said, "What's the big deal?"

Crabs in a hurry, scuttle like pros,
They steal my chips as the sea breeze blows.
I shout, "Hey, wait! That's my lunch!"
But they just cocked their eyes, saying, "You're a hunch!"

Shells and treasures scattered around,
Each step I take, I'm more falling down.
The waves giggle softly, as I lose my grip,
The ocean's my friend, but I just did a flip!

With footprints behind that come and go,
I ponder life choices as tides ebb slow.
I'm all about fun, at least that's my rhyme,
Counting the laughs, not just the time.

Beyond the Salt and Sun

Under the sun, I'm a golden fry,
I roasted myself, oh me, oh my.
My friends all laugh, they toss me a shade,
While I shimmer away in this heat parade.

I spotted a dolphin, thought it was sweet,
Then it splashed me hard, oh what a treat!
I sloshed and swayed, my drink taking flight,
Now I'm wet and wild, a slippery sight!

Building a sand tower, tall as my dreams,
It crumbled fast; my hopes, it deems.
But a kid with a bucket offered a plan,
"Let's build a boat"—now we're sailing, man!

So here's to life, while we laugh and play,
With waves for a band, we dance the day.
In moments of joy, there's always a pun,
To be silly and free, beyond the salt and sun!

The Coral's Melancholy Ballad

Beneath the waves, they gather round,
A coral choir with no sound.
They wiggle and jiggle in their sea dress,
Hoping for fish but getting no less.

A jellyfish floats, in a comical sway,
"I can't move fast!" he shouts, in dismay.
But when he stings, in a bellyful wriggle,
You'd laugh too, if you saw him giggle.

Anemones wave, with dramatic flair,
They clutch little fish, in their locked stare.
"Come here, my dear!" they call with a cheer,
But the fish just swim off, with a wink and a sneer.

A starfish grumbles, "Where's my right arm?"
"You lost it to dinner!" says a crab with charm.
In this underwater circus, jesters abound,
With laughter and currents, joy can be found.

Fragments of Shells and Time

In the sand, there lies a shoe,
A crab appears and claims it's new.
"What style! What flair!" he struts about,
While beachgoers stare, with giggles devout.

Conch shells whisper secrets of yore,
"Heard you dated an octopus? Tell us more!"
"Oh please!" she sighs, rolling her eye,
"That sucker's got eight, I can't even try!"

A seagull dances on one leg,
While fishing for crumbs, he starts to beg.
"Oh, what a ruckus, life as a bird!"
But he trips on a wave, and his laughter is heard!

Pebbles giggle as they tumble in time,
Each one a joke, each one a rhyme.
With tides that tease and sands that shift,
The beach is a stage, where jokes are a gift.

Heartbeats of the Ocean's Edge

The waves come crashing with a slap,
A dolphin jumps, and what a flap!
"I'm the captain!" he splashes with glee,
While seagulls squawk, "Not without me!"

Starfish lounge, pretending to nap,
"Let's throw a party!" yells one with a cap.
But party or not, they're stuck on the floor,
While beach balls bounce and the children explore.

Crabs in tuxedos, they scuttle and sway,
Dancing to rhythms the tide won't replay.
"Join us!" they say, "in our gala of fun!"
But when they get pinched, it's a dash and a run.

A mermaid peeks, her scales full of spark,
"What's this? A landslide?" with a laugh and a snark.
The ocean hums, like a fun carnival,
With heartbeats of laughter, it enchants us all.

The Unseen World Below the Surface

Bubbles rise up, like secrets untold,
Where fish wear hats and get called bold.
"Look at me swim!" boasts a clownfish bright,
"I'm the funniest fish, in day or in night!"

An octopus joins, with eight limbs in play,
"Who needs a partner? I'm fine my way!"
He juggles some shells, quite the odd sight,
While a shrimp just chuckles, filled with delight.

A lobster sings low, with a voice like a bar,
"Underwater karaoke's where we are!"
With every note, he rocks the deep sea,
While the eels sway along, in rhythmic glee.

In the hush of the depths, jokes bubble and flow,
In a world where laughter's set to aglow.
So if you dive down, give a wink and a cheer,
For below the surface, there's always good humor near.

Walking the Line Between Sky and Sea

There once was a seagull, quite a charmer,
He wore a tiny hat and a floating armor.
He danced with the waves, a sight to behold,
While stealing my fries, being cheeky and bold.

The crabs held a meeting, quite serious, you see,
Debating if they should join the seagull's spree.
They scuttled in suits, with a pinstripe flair,
Looking for snacks and some salty air.

A fish flipped and flopped, aiming for fame,
He wanted a selfie, oh, what a claim!
But slipped on a clam, a splash and a splash,
Now he's just known for his comical crash.

At sunset they gather, the oddest of crew,
With laughter and stories, they shared quite a few.
So here's to the antics by surf and by breeze,
Where silliness reigns, and everyone's pleased.

A Symphony of Wind and Water

The waves sing a tune, a screechy delight,
While seaweed performs in the shimmering light.
A crab with a kazoo joins the chorus quite loud,
While dolphins leap by, gathering a crowd.

The breeze played the flute, it giggled and swayed,
As a fish in a bow tie showed off in the shade.
Turtles tapped softly, keeping the beat,
With jellyfish twirling on oh-so-light feet.

A whale tried to waltz but fell on his tail,
Creating a splash that told quite the tale.
The gulls in the back tossed popcorn around,
Making the concert a real hoot and sound.

So laugh in the light of a starry-gold night,
Where music of nature is pure sheer delight.
In the symphony grand, no one's too stiff,
For the ocean joins in with a whimsical riff.

Tidal Serenades of the Heart

Under the sun, where the water shimmers bright,
A crab fell in love, what a hilarious sight!
He serenaded a starfish with all of his might,
But she just rolled her eyes and said, 'Not tonight!'

The waves whispered secrets, their frothy confessions,
While clams played poker, making strange impressions.
Seagulls squawked loudly, calling out names,
While the fish in the schools were playing their games.

A dolphin gave chase, wanting to befriend,
But tripped on a surfboard, oh, what a blend!
The laughter erupted, as tides came to play,
Summoning joy in a wave of ballet.

So raise up a shell and toast to the sands,
Where creatures of whimsy share joyous bands.
For in this grand ocean, laughter reigns supreme,
Creating a rhythm like none can redeem.

Collecting Stories from Stormy Skies

A thundercloud grumbled, 'What makes me mad?'
'The fishermen's gossip, it drives me quite bad!'
He hurled down some rain to spoil the parade,
Yet fish in slick suits just danced and displayed.

With each drop that fell, a tale to be spun,
'Who knew clouds had drama? Now that's really fun!'
Lightning sparked laughter as everyone fled,
While turtlenecks fashioned went swimming instead.

A pirate ship sailed, but all were aghast,
For the crew had misplaced their very last flask.
Now soggy and sloppy, they searched high and low,
While the rain kept on teasing, 'Oh where did it go?'

So next time you ponder a storm rolling near,
Remember the tales and hold on to your cheer.
For nature's a jester when skies turn to gray,
And laughter can brighten the dullest of days.

The Ocean's Breath in Quiet Moments

The sea sighs softly, a lazy tune,
As jellyfish dance like balloons in June.
Crabs in bow ties scuttle about,
While seagulls gossip, full of clout.

Little fish giggle, what a sight,
As dolphins jump for pure delight.
Tide pools chuckle, a secret grin,
Inviting us all to just dive in.

Harmonies of Sea and Sky

Clouds puffed up like frothy cream,
While the sun winks in a golden dream.
Seashells whisper jests of old,
As we chase them, brave and bold.

A crab plays fetch with a beach troll,
While windsurfers pursue their goal.
The horizon giggles with each splash,
Making seaweed wigs in a dash.

The Unruly Waves' Edge

Waves in a hurry, they tumble and roll,
Laughing like children, they take a toll.
Surfboards crash with a comical splat,
As the ocean shouts, 'You're flat as a mat!'

Seagulls wheel with a cheeky grace,
As fish tease them, making a race.
The beach is a carnival, laughter, and cheer,
With sandcastles toppling from reflections unclear.

Forgotten Wonders Beneath the Surface

Beneath the waves, a treasure chest,
With rubber ducks vying for the best.
An octopus juggles with flair and style,
While clownfish join in, with a grin and a smile.

Sea cucumbers strut in a funny parade,
As starfish wink, their plans well laid.
Coral reefs giggle, colors so bright,
Holding a disco beneath the moonlight.

Tides of Time and Memory

Waves crash loud, but I stand still,
Snatching shells, oh what a thrill!
The tide rolled in with a slap and a grin,
I lost my shoes, but let the fun begin!

Seagulls caw with a cheeky tone,
Swooping down to steal my cone.
I laugh as they dance, a silly ballet,
As I chase them off, all in good play!

Each wave pulls back, a mischievous tease,
I stumble and trip—oh, where's my keys?
The ocean's a trickster, plays peek-a-boo,
With sand in my shorts, I'll still bid adieu!

In the sunset glow, my worries unwind,
As I pretend to be a sailor, unconfined.
With salt in the air and humor to spare,
This shore will always have memories to share.

Serendipity at the Water's Edge

Strolling along, where the sand meets the sea,
I spotted a crab, oh what glee!
He waved his claws, a quirky little dance,
I joined in, thinking I had a chance!

A beach ball flew by, not a soul in sight,
I kicked it back with all of my might.
Instead, it wedged between two tall rocks,
Now I'm the talk of all beachy gocks!

Flip-flops flop as I run for a catch,
My sunhat flies off—oh what a match!
With waves at my feet and laughter around,
This paradise feels somethin' profound!

Just past the tide-line, where wonders abound,
I find a note: "You've been crowned the clown!"
With serendipitous joy, I dance in delight,
The beach is my kingdom, a whimsical sight!

Lighthouses and Lost Lovers

I climbed the tower, my heart all aglow,
In search of a lover, but where did he go?
The beacon shone bright, but my heart's on the run,
Couldn't find him—so I turned for some fun!

Rocks below me, as slick as can be,
I slipped and I giggled, oh look at me!
A lighthouse so sturdy, but my grip's not so right,
Caught in a tumble, oh what a sight!

Messages sent with bottles and care,
Each one a story, but where's my pair?
The waves whisper secrets, oh how they tease,
While I tripped on my hopes, like old castles of cheese!

In saltwater laughter, I find my way,
With lighthouses guiding, I'll be okay.
For love may be lost, like my sandwich today,
But I'll feast on this joy—come what may!

The Siren's Lament upon the Rocks

A siren sings from her rock so high,
But her song's for the fishes, not a sailor nearby.
She waves at the gulls, who just laugh in return,
While her tail flops around, oh how we yearn!

"Come hither, my lovelies!" she sings out with glee,
But the fishermen smile; they can't swim to thee!
Her hair's like seaweed; it's tangled in knots,
And her shell collection? Well, it's full of old thoughts!

On calm sunny days, she tries to impress,
With dances of bubbles and a glittering dress.
But with each crashing wave, she's swept out to sea,
Just looking for mates, like a beach party!

So here's to the siren, who calls from the shore,
Outwitting her heart and longing for more.
With a twirl and a splash, she'll forever remain,
A creature of laughter—fondness, not pain!

Salty Secrets Beneath the Waves

Fish gossip all day, in a watery bog,
They chuckle and wiggle, over a log.
Crabs throw a party, with shells left and right,
Whispers of seaweed, oh what a sight!

Starfish play chess, with eyes all aglow,
While dolphins giggle, putting on a show.
A mermaid sings tunes, that tickle the tide,
With sea turtles dancing, she'll be their guide!

Barnacles grumble, stuck firm to the floor,
They mumble their secrets, forever more.
Each wave is a laugh, a playful embrace,
In the depths of the blue, there's always a trace.

Dance of the Crashing Surf

Waves jump and tumble, a wild ballet,

Seagulls take flight, then forget their way.

Sandy toes shuffle, as shells start to sing,

A clam takes a bow, oh what a grand fling!

The tide rolls in, with a whoosh and a splat,

A starfish decides it needs a new hat.

Jellyfish waltz, with grace all their own,

While crabs tap their claws, like they've found a throne.

Laughter erupts, from the children nearby,

As waves tickle toes and seagulls fly high.

Life's a big party, with no need to fuss,

In the dance of the surf, come join all of us!

Horizon's Embrace at Dusk

As sun dips below, the sky paints a grin,

Dolphins delight, with their shiny fin.

Stars start to spark, in the dusky parade,

While crabs set the mood, in their shell-made shade.

A beach ball gets lost, in the warm salty breeze,

While tourists play catch, and forget where they sneezed.

Moonbeams bring laughs, along with the tide,

As ancient sea tales get shared with pride.

The horizon whispers, "Do come sit with me,"

As night plays its song, in harmonious glee.

The world's on a edge, but we roll with the jest,

For in this great ballet, we're all truly blessed.

Shoreline Dreams and Starlit Skies

Upon the beach, where dreams start to rise,

The sand holds our secrets, beneath starlit skies.

Seashells collect wishes, sweet hopes they embrace,

As waves tell tall tales, of a faraway place.

Laughter echoes loud, in the cool evening air,

While crabs race the tide, without any care.

With flip-flops in hand, we dance through the night,

Under the moon's glow, everything feels right.

Fish swimming in circles, with golden delight,

Create a spectacle, that's simply out of sight.

In this magical realm, where waves play and glide,

We find joy in each tide, together we ride.

Tales Carried by the Maritime Wind

A seagull swoops with a squawk,
Stealing fries from that old dock.
Captain Bob yells with a grin,
"Hey there! That's where my lunch has been!"

Fish all gathered, doing the jig,
Wearing sunglasses, feeling quite big.
A crab points left, then he points right,
"Who borrowed my shell? What a silly sight!"

Mermaids giggle in coral gowns,
Swapping tales of all the clowns.
With treasure maps and sneaky traps,
"Where'd all the sunken chests go? Oh, snaps!"

So raise your glass, enjoy the breeze,
Maritime tales put hearts at ease.
For life's a wave, just catch your flow,
And dance in the sand—let the laughter glow!

Solitude Beneath the Sailor's Star

In the moonlight, a lone boat sways,
While fish join in for a splashing ballet.
The captain, lost in a barrel of rum,
Ponders if crabs are better than scum!

Stars above twinkle, wear a grin,
As waves clap hands, no need to pretend.
The jellyfish float with a jelly-like grace,
"Why so serious? It's a party place!"

A dolphin leaps, makes a splashy mistake,
A flipsy-flopsy mid-sea break.
"Oops," he chuckles, "that's not my best,
Maybe this ocean's not for the jest!"

So sail on by, let laughter be,
For every wave holds a silly spree.
Under stars shining bright and far,
Adventure lies, followed by a bizarre!

A Whispered Promise from the Deep

The octopus waves with eight long arms,
Says, "I know all the ocean's charms!"
A sailor laughs, "Can you fix my boat?"
"Sure, but first let's have a float!"

Crabs and clownfish throw a ball,
Kicking up sand, splashes for all.
Mermaids swim by, sing out a tune,
"Who's ready to dance under the moon?"

A treasure chest opens with a creaky sigh,
Revealing old socks from a fisherman guy.
"Guess that's not gold, but hey, I don't mind,
We'll start a new fashion with treasures we find!"

So dive in deep, find joy in the blue,
With whispers of laughter and giggles anew.
Beneath the ripples, life's a delight,
With every wave comes a new silly sight!

Chasing the Evening's Limelight

As the sun dips low, that glorious gold,
The jellybeans roll, their secrets retold.
"Where's my candy?" a pirate cries loud,
"Swab the deck—it's a jellybean crowd!"

A pelican struts with a swagger so grand,
Sporting a hat from a nearby stand.
"Is this a party? Can I join the dance?"
With flippers and fin, he joins at a chance!

The tides start to giggle, waves start to sway,
Seagulls join in, singing all day.
A crab snaps his claws, "Let's make a toast,
To seafarer shenanigans! We're having the most!"

So beneath the sunset, let laughter abound,
For life on the sea is joy that's profound.
In every ripple, kindness shines bright,
Chasing the evening's glowing light!

www.ingramcontent.com/pod-product-compliance
Lightning Source LLC
Chambersburg PA
CBHW072217070526
44585CB00015B/1380